How Does Your Garden Grow?

David Keystone

Carole Coburn

How Does Your Garden Grow?

Text: David Keystone and Carole Coburn
Editor: Cameron Macintosh
Design: Georgie Wilson
Illustrations: Rae Dale
Photographs: Lindsay Edwards
Reprint: Siew Han Ong

Acknowledgements
The authors and publisher would like to acknowledge permission to reproduce material from the following sources:
Photographs by Australian Picture Library/ John & Lorraine Carnemolla, p.14 bottom; Auscape/ C.Andrew, pp.13 left, 13 bottom right, 15/ Kathie Atkinson, pp. 13 top right, 13 bottom centre/ Wayne Lawler, p.13 bottom left; Lindsay Edwards, front cover, back cover;pp.4, 5, 9, 10-11, 12, 18, 20, 21, 22, 23; Getty Images/ Stone, p.13 top centre; Imagen/ Bill Thomas, p.14 top.

PM Extras Non-Fiction
Emerald
How Does Your Garden Grow?
Working with Wood
How Magic Tricks Work
Junk Srculpture
Spin, Weave, Knit and Knot
The Puppet Show

Text © 2004 Cengage Learning Australia Pty Limited
Illustrations © 2004 Cengage Learning Australia Pty Limited

For product information and technology assistance,
in Australia call 1300 790 853;
in New Zealand call 0508 635 766

For permission to use material from this text or product,
please email **aust.permissions@cengage.com**

ISBN 978 0 17 011439 4
ISBN 978 0 17 011434 9 (set)

Cengage Learning Australia
Level 7, 80 Dorcas Street
South Melbourne, Victoria Australia 3205

Cengage Learning New Zealand
Unit 4B Rosedale Office Park
331 Rosedale Road, Albany, North Shore NZ 0632

For learning solutions, visit **cengage.com.au**

Printed in Australia by Ligare Pty Ltd
17 18 19 23 22 21

Contents

Introduction

Daniel, Ismini and Natasha sat eating their lunch outside their classroom. They looked around the yard. It was very bare. There were no shady trees to sit under. Only a few weeds grew here and there.

Erica came past them pushing a wheelbarrow. Erica was the school gardener. She maintained the gardens around the school and taught the children about caring for the environment. She was helping to **landscape** the front of the school. It now had a grassed area and shrubs.

As Erica pushed the wheelbarrow towards the front gate, Natasha had an idea. "Erica said you can make a garden anywhere with the right tools and plants. Perhaps we could make one here at school."

Daniel and Ismini thought this was a fantastic idea.

"My mum made her own garden," said Daniel. "We all helped her."

They talked about Daniel's garden and who did the different tasks to create it. It wasn't very hard if you knew what to do.

They decided to ask Erica to help them make a garden in the school grounds.

Design a Garden

Erica really liked the children's idea. "Why don't you design the garden yourselves?" she asked them. "Start by planning it on paper. Add the plants you would like, and other things such as paths or rocks."

The children had lots of great ideas for the garden.

Favourite plants
and labels

Animal life —
butterflies, bees, birds

Shade

Non-living things
— paths, rocks

Flowers
and leaves

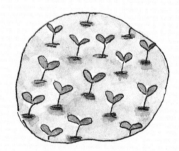

Patterns

The children eagerly told Erica their ideas. Erica was impressed! She suggested using a list of these ideas to plan the new garden.

The children made a list of the things they liked most, and with Erica's help they agreed on a design for the garden.

Our garden and what we like

- colourful flowers
- shade
- insects and birds
- places to hide
- curved flower border
- sweet smell of ginger lilies

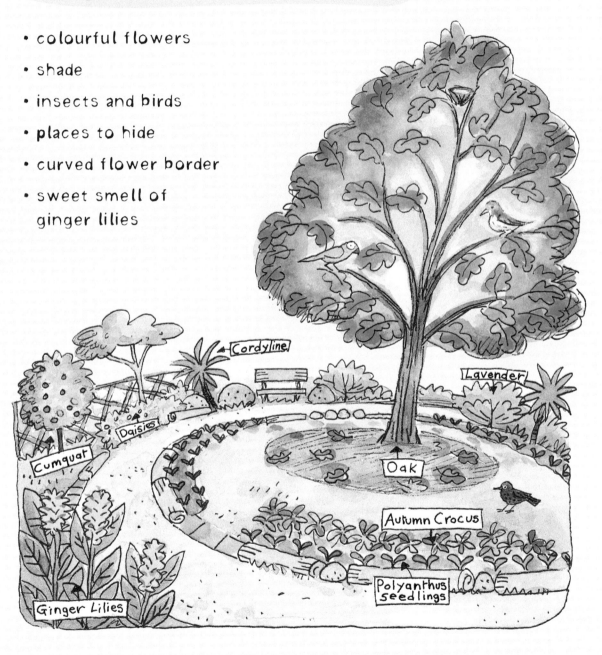

Cordyline

Lavender

Daisies

Cumquat

Oak

Autumn Crocus

Ginger Lilies

Polyanthus seedlings

Tool Shed

"Working in a garden is much easier when you use the correct tools," explained Erica, as she opened the shed door. The children stared at the range of tools. "We need to get the soil ready for planting," she said. "I've drawn some tools that we need to use, to perform different jobs. I've written some information about each tool."

Erica's list of tools

spade a flat blade with a handle for digging and cutting through soil

garden fork a short handle with teeth to break up the soil and make holes

wheelbarrow a wheeled vehicle for carrying things easily

rake a long handle with teeth, for smoothing the soil

hand fork a short handle with tines for breaking up soil

hand trowel a short handle and blade for making holes for plants

bulb planter a cylinder with a handle for cutting soil, making holes and planting bulbs

gloves worn to protect your hands

"Will we use all these tools in the garden?" asked Daniel.

"You'll be able to use most of them, but there are some tools that are used only by adults," said Erica. "These tools have sharp blades. A lot of care needs to be taken when using them."

Adults Only Tools

Secateurs garden scissors used for pruning plants

Clippers flat blade garden scissors used for trimming

Preparing the Soil

"Plants need loose, crumbly soil so that their roots can spread easily under the ground," explained Erica. "Fine root hairs absorb water and **nutrients** from the loose soil."

Daniel and Natasha used their feet to push the spades and garden forks into the ground. These tools were good levers to break up the soil. Erica was busy slicing up weeds with a spade. Ismini helped pile them into the wheelbarrow.

"Weeds can be turned into compost to feed our garden," said Erica. "We won't waste anything."

They all worked very hard, digging the ground.

"This soil is sandy. It's easy to dig," said Natasha, resting against her spade.

"Yes," replied Erica. "Plants will grow quickly here but the soil will dry out rapidly. We need to make it more spongy."

Chapter 5
2nd Month

Nutrients for the Soil

Compost heap

"Compost will help improve our soil," said Erica. "Compost is mostly a mixture of plant and vegetable waste. A compost heap breaks down this waste. The waste rots and eventually becomes **humus**. Humus is a good fertiliser for plants."

Natasha dug the soil lightly. Daniel placed the plastic compost bin over the soil. "Now we will put these weeds in and add some grass clippings," he said.

"Here's a bucket of food scraps we've been collecting in class," said Ismini.

"That's a great idea," said Erica. "We need to add waste to our compost every day."

"We make compost at home," said Natasha. "I noticed lots of tiny animals in the humus when Mum was spreading it around her plants."

"Healthy compost is a home for many living things," said Erica. "Microscopic living things such as bacteria break it down. They're called micro-organisms. These pictures show some of them. And some bigger creatures help, too. You can spot these in most composts."

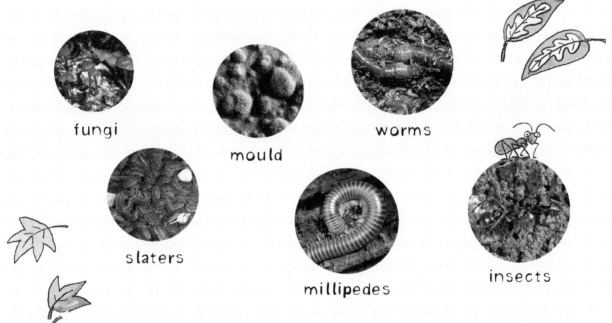

fungi

mould

worms

slaters

millipedes

insects

"When we recycle all our scraps we cut down on our waste collection," said Erica.

"And it doesn't cost us money to make our compost," added Daniel.

"It helps to improve the soil, too," said Erica. "Every gardener knows how good compost is for a garden."

Worm farm

"Here's something else that will help our soil," said Erica, taking the top off a round box. The children looked in to see hundreds of wriggling worms.

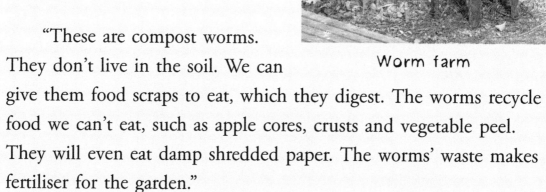

Worm farm

"These are compost worms. They don't live in the soil. We can give them food scraps to eat, which they digest. The worms recycle food we can't eat, such as apple cores, crusts and vegetable peel. They will even eat damp shredded paper. The worms' waste makes fertiliser for the garden."

One of the round boxes was sitting on top of the other. The top one, where the worms live, had a lid and drainage holes so that any extra liquid could drain into the bottom box.

"Worms like a cool, moist and dark **habitat**," said Erica. "We need to add a piece of sack over their food and a daily squirt of water with a spray bottle. The worms will soon be breeding again. Our garden will have rich, spongy soil when we mix in the **worm castings**."

Worm castings

Plants from Plants

Natasha had brought a clump of Iris to school.
"Mum said we can divide this plant up into a few
smaller plants for our garden," she said.

Iris

"Yes," said Erica. "We can make new plants
from other plants. We call this plant propagation.
We can propagate new plants in many ways.
Let me show you how."

Erica used a spade to cut the plant into several pieces. "As long
as each piece has roots it will grow," she said. "Plant each piece in a
pot with some **potting mix**, and water it well. We'll grow them in
pots until we're ready to plant them in the garden."

New plants from cuttings

"We can also take cuttings from different shrubs in the garden," said Erica. "We'll take some soft wood cuttings from the green stems. This is how we do it."

Step 1

Cut a stem from a shrub. Each stem needs to have about four leaf nodes. A node is a lump on the stem where a new shoot will grow.

Remove the bottom leaves and cut the stem just below the last node. Place the cutting in a plastic bag.

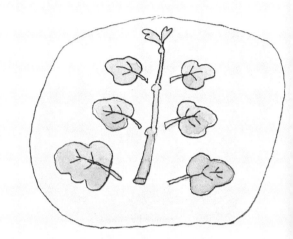

Step 2

Fill small pots with potting mix. Use a pencil to poke a hole in the mix. Place your cutting in the hole. Label your pot with the name of the plant, and the date.

Step 3

Water your cuttings
immediately. Poke three sticks
into the pot to make a frame
around the cuttings. Cover it
with plastic. This keeps the
moisture in. Keep the pots out
of the sun but in a well lit
place. Check the cuttings
weekly and water them if the
soil dries out.

Step 4

Check if your cuttings have
taken root. Be gentle. If roots
have grown, take off the
plastic. Let it grow for at least
three weeks in the pot. It
needs a strong root system to
grow in the garden.

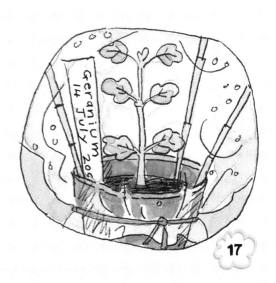

Planting Day

When there were many strong roots on the plants, Erica knew that the plants were strong enough to survive in the garden. The children were really excited about seeing all the plants in their garden for the first time.

"Let's place the plants where we want them before we plant them," suggested Erica. "We'll make certain that they have room to grow."

With the plants laid out in the garden, Erica demonstrated how a potted plant is planted in the ground.

How to plant

Step 1

Use a hand trowel to dig a hole wider than the pot.

Step 2

Tap the pot to loosen the root ball and slide the plant out gently.

Step 3

Place the plant in the hole. Check that it is sitting in the soil at the same level as it sat in the pot.

Step 4

Fill the hole with soil. Press the soil firmly and gently around the plant.

Step 5

Generously water each plant immediately.

Planting seeds

Ismini had a packet of poppy flower seeds. They were sealed to keep them fresh. Daniel had a paper bag of seed pods which was splitting and leaking seeds.

Erica laughed. "I have a tongue twister. Seeds stirred into sifted sand are simple to scatter." She mixed the seeds into a bucket of sand, and handed it to Daniel.

"You can easily see where the seeds have landed," said Daniel, as he sprinkled the sand and seeds over the bare ground. The children covered the seeds with a fine layer of garden soil.

"We need to keep the soil moist until the seedlings are fairly tall," advised Erica.

Planting bulbs

Natasha had some daffodil **bulbs** from her garden. Bulbs can be divided every year. "They multiply under the ground," said Erica.

Erica showed the children how to plant bulbs using a bulb planter. "This tool cuts a hole in the ground. It then removes a plug of soil inside it. Place the bulb, pointy end up, into the hole."

"Now," said Erica. "Squeeze the handle on the planter so that the soil falls on top of the bulb."

"I never thought planting bulbs would be so easy," said Daniel.

Caring for the Garden

The group was very keen to observe what happened to their garden.

"After all your hard work," asked Erica, "how will you make certain that the garden is well cared for?"

"It's really important to keep the plants in our garden healthy and strong," said Daniel. "I'll make sure we add compost to the garden."

"I'll start a garden diary," said Natasha. "We can write about what works for us and what happens in our garden."

"We could ask others to help water the plants, especially during the school holidays," said Ismini. "Maybe we could put in a sprinkler system with a timer. Then we would know for sure that our garden will get watered."

"That sounds like a great idea," said Erica. "We need to cover the bare soil with **mulch**, too. Putting mulch on the soil will stop it drying out quickly."

They all spread mulch over most of the garden. The thick carpet of mulch looked much better than the bare ground they had started with.

Then Ismini said, "How about we list all the different jobs? Each of us can choose a job to do. I'll write a name next to each one."

List of gardening jobs

Pruning - Erica

Tidying - Daniel

Fertilising - Natasha

Compost bin - Daniel

Tools - Everyone

Mulching - Erica

Worm farm - Ismini

Diary - Natasha

Watering roster - Ismini

Finished Garden

"Isn't this great?" said Erica. "After all our hard work, our garden looks better than we ever imagined."

"I'm sad our garden is finished," said Ismini. "It was so much fun designing and making it. It's starting to look very green, and buds and daisies are starting to appear."

Dear Erica, Daniel, Ismini and Natasha,

We love your new garden. We were wondering if you could help us to design and create a garden, too.

From Mrs Taylor and Grade 3.

"But Ismini," replied Erica, "a garden is never finished. It keeps changing and growing. We can do so much to help it – collect seeds and strike cuttings from our own plants. We can compost the dead flowers and leaves, and of course we can sit here in the shade and just enjoy it."

So Erica, Daniel, Ismini and Natasha did just that!